FOURTH and GOAL

A RECRUITING PLAYBOOK FOR FOOTBALL PARENTS

JULIET JONES PETTIJOHN
& DUKE PETTIJOHN

Table of Contents

Introduction
Welcome to the Recruiting Journey

By Juliet Jones Pettijohn & Duke Pettijohn

If you're reading this, you're probably a parent standing at the edge of an exciting but overwhelming process: your athlete is being recruited. Maybe they've just started getting interest from schools, maybe the offers are coming in, or maybe you're just trying to figure out how to get your athlete noticed in the first place.

Whatever stage you're in, you've probably already felt the whirlwind — late-night Hudl edits, frantic travel planning for camps, the excitement of that first coach DM, and the pressure to "do it right." This journey can be exhilarating, but it can also feel confusing and stressful — especially if you've never been through it before.

Here's the good news: you are not alone, and there *is* a way to approach this process with confidence. The recruiting process isn't just about where your athlete plays in college — it's also about who they become along the way. Done well, it can teach them discipline, resilience, communication skills, and how to handle both success and adversity.

I remember the day our son's recruiting journey really took off — and I remember feeling ecstatic and a bit anxious.

Suddenly, the phone calls and texts started coming in from area coaches and recruiters. Our mailbox filled with camp invitations, questionnaires, and "just checking in" messages. I didn't know who half these coaches were, what role they played in an offer decision, or even which conference some of these schools belonged to.

In those early days, I created a spreadsheet with columns for everything: school name, conference, head coach, city, and date of first contact. I kept it up for a few weeks, but as the interest grew, the calls and visits multiplied, and my careful organization fell apart. Pretty soon, I was just winging it — which worked some days and left me panicked on others.

Over time, I learned to give myself permission to ask questions — of other parents, of recruiters, and coaches — and to build a network of families who were going through the same thing. The more I listened and shared, the more confident I became.

This guide is what I wish I'd had back then: a playbook for parents. It won't eliminate every stress or answer every single question, but it will give you a framework — a way to stay organized, keep perspective, and enjoy what can truly be one of the most exciting seasons in your athlete's life.

This guide is here to help you:

- Understand your athlete's role and responsibility — so you can empower them to own their journey.
- Find your lane as a parent — balancing support with letting them lead.
- Communicate effectively with your athlete and with coaches.
- Navigate NIL safely and wisely — without getting lost in the noise.
- Prepare for visits, commitments, and signing day — so nothing takes you by surprise.

Think of this as your sideline playbook. You don't need to memorize every detail right now — just know where to look when you need answers.

Most of all, remember this should be fun! Recruiting is an opportunity to celebrate your athlete's hard work, not just survive the process. Our goal is to help you and your family enjoy the ride!

Chapter 1

Your Athlete's Responsibility

Sometimes, as parents, we try so hard to manage everything for our children that we forget this is actually their journey, not ours.

I knew our son was ready for the challenge of achieving his goal of playing at a Power 5 school the day I received a call from an athletic trainer. The conversation went something like this:

"Mrs. Pettijohn, this is Nate from Crull Fitness. Your son Riley's been training here for a few months, and I was wondering if you could provide a method of payment."

That single call told me everything I needed to know — Riley was taking ownership. He had not only found the trainer on his own, but he also figured out how to get to the training facility without ever asking his parents for help.

In that moment, I realized he wasn't just preparing for his next football season — he was forging his own path to become a top recruit. He was showing us, and himself, that this dream truly belonged to him.

Perspective and Practical Advice

As legendary coach Bear Bryant once said, "Don't try to live your life through your kids — they need to make their own mistakes."

Your job is to set the environment for success — not to drag them toward it. If you constantly must ride your athlete about completing assignments, watching film, studying for exams, or learning their playbook, it may be time for an honest conversation about effort versus expectations. This same standard applies to their diet and sleep habits: as parents, you can commit to providing balanced meals, supplements, specialty trainers, and even a strength program — but your athlete must have skin in the game by following through.

And don't get it twisted — grades still come first! Without good grades, your athlete risks eligibility and may take themselves out of the running for top schools before a coach ever calls. Responsibility in the classroom is just as important as responsibility on the field.

Action Checklist for Athletes

☑ Lead Your Own Process: Schedule your workouts, watch film, study your playbook, and communicate with your high school coaches and recruiting coaches yourself.

☑ Own Your Habits: Stay on top of assignments, get adequate sleep, and stick to the nutrition plan your parents provide.

☑ Show Initiative: Don't wait to be reminded — update your Hudl highlights, use social media to share your progress and success, ask for feedback from coaches/trainers, and take pride in doing the little things right.

Chapter 2
The Parent's Role

If Chapter 1 was about putting the responsibility where it belongs — on your athlete — then this chapter is about defining what your role really is as a parent. Tony Dungy once shared "You can't coach character, but you can model it. The best thing you can do for a young athlete is give them the tools and space to grow."

Duke played at Syracuse during its glory days — and it goes without saying that the football world is very small, often just one degree of separation. I'm sure at times it was hard for him not to take over the process completely. There were moments we wanted to jump in and email or text coaches ourselves when Riley hesitated or forgot.

But we learned quickly that if we did the talking, coaches wouldn't get to know him — they'd just know us. And at the next level, we won't be there to answer their texts, emails, or calls.

As parents, we are the guardrails, not the driver. Our job is to create an environment where our athletes can thrive — emotionally, academically, and physically — without taking over the steering wheel.

Supporting Without Overstepping

It's natural to want to help, but there's a fine line between support and control.

- Provide Structure: Create a household routine that allows time for training, recovery, homework, and rest.
- Encourage Communication: Help your athlete draft messages or guide conversations with coaches, but let them be the one to send and speak.
- Stay Neutral: Avoid projecting your dream school onto them — let them form their own opinions on where they fit best.

Being the Emotional Anchor

Recruiting can be an emotional rollercoaster. There will be highs (offers, visits) and lows (injuries, no callbacks).

- Model Composure: Don't panic when there's a setback; show your athlete how to handle disappointment and keep moving forward.
- Celebrate the Work, Not Just Results: Praise effort and character, not just wins or offers.
- Be the Safe Space: Sometimes your athlete just needs to vent without getting a lecture.

Advocacy vs. Enabling

You are your child's first advocate — but be careful not to turn into their manager.

- Step In When Needed: If a situation is unsafe, unethical, or exploitative, you step in — otherwise, let them handle the day-to-day.

- Teach Problem-Solving: When they forget to respond to a coach, don't bail them out. Let them feel the consequence, then encourage them to fix it.

Action Checklist for Parents

☑ Create Structure: Set a consistent routine for schoolwork, training, meals, and sleep.

☑ Coach Communication: Role-play coach calls, review texts/emails, or help them outline talking points — then step back and let them take the lead.

☑ Stay Objective: Keep a journal or spreadsheet to track offers, visits, and communications so decisions are made on facts, not emotions.

Chapter 3
Communication & Relationships

———————— • ————————

Coach Mike Tomlin reminds us that good teams communicate, but great teams build relationships. The same goes for parents and athletes – communication is just the first step; trust and connection are what take the journey to the next level! One of the most overlooked parts of the recruiting process isn't speed, size, or stats — it's communication. And in today's environment, social media – especially X – is a powerful tool for athletes. Used correctly, it allows them to communicate with schools, engage fan bases, and increase visibility with other programs. Every post reflects on your athlete, so professionalism, consistency, and positivity are key. Coaches are looking for athletes who are not only talented but also respectful, responsive, and proactive!

Helping Your Athlete Own the Process

Recruiting is a chance for your athlete to practice life skills that will matter far beyond football: professionalism, initiative, and follow-through. Sit with your athlete to draft messages, role-play calls, and encourage timely follow-ups. Conversely, pay close attention to how a program communicates with your athlete. The frequency, tone, and effort they put into staying in touch are direct reflections of their level of interest and investment in your athlete.

The Parent's Role

Parents have an important role — but it's easy to unintentionally dominate the process. Be present, ask big-picture questions, and respect coaches' timelines.

Allowing Relationships to Develop Naturally

Not every coach or staff will be a perfect fit — and that's okay. Depending on the number of offers, connection may weigh more heavily in the final decision. With more offers, be selective. With fewer, proactively engage to build momentum. Know your message and practice sharing it consistently.

Strong communication skills do more than impress coaches — they help reveal how the staff plans to use and develop your athlete. These conversations shed light on whether the program envisions your athlete as a key individual contributor, a long-term team leader, or a role-specific player. Understanding this can be pivotal when weighing multiple offers and deciding which environment best aligns with their growth.

Staying Organized

Track dead periods, save contacts so you know who is calling/texting, log all communication, and set reminders for calls and visits so that nothing slips through the cracks.

Quick-Action Checklist

Draft first coach email or text message with athlete (have them send)

- Practice phone call conversations
- Build recruiting communication spreadsheet
- Respond to coaches within 24 hours
- Write down 3–4 key messages to share consistently
- Track which programs feel like the best fit

Chapter 4
Navigating NIL With Confidence

———— • ————

When NIL (Name, Image, and Likeness) rules first changed in 2021, they opened a brand-new world for student-athletes — and an equally big challenge for parents. Suddenly, your child might have the chance to make money from their personal brand before they ever step foot on a college campus. That's exciting — but also daunting to understand and navigate.

From our own experience, we learned something valuable during Riley's recruiting process. On both unofficial and official visits, schools scheduled time to discuss NIL compensation. Riley chose not to participate in those conversations. His priority was selecting a program based on fit, development, and opportunity—not money.

There were times when coaches shared NIL projections directly, and as parents, we stepped in to handle those discussions so schools could understand his value compared with other programs. Ultimately, Riley committed without ever knowing what his final compensation would be.

Not every family can or should approach it this way, and there's no one "right" decision. Still, in a world driven by money, we're proud he stayed focused on what truly mattered to him.

This chapter will help you understand what NIL means, what to watch out for, and how to set your athlete up for success.

1. NIL 101 for Parents

At its simplest, NIL means athletes can profit from their name, image, and likeness. This could include:

- Social Media Posts – Paid promotions or shoutouts
- Camps and Clinics – Running their own or working others'
- Merchandise – Selling shirts, hats, or personal gear
- Appearances – Paid signings, meet-and-greets, speaking events

But NIL doesn't mean "free money" — and it doesn't mean every athlete will get six-figure deals. Parents need to help their athletes stay grounded while staying open to opportunity.

2. Legal, Compliance & Reporting

The NIL space is still young and constantly evolving, and rules can vary by state and school district.

- Follow the Rules – Some states limit NIL activity for high school athletes, so check your state's athletic association website before signing anything.
- Avoid Shady Offers – If a deal sounds too good to be true, it probably is. Don't sign contracts without reading the fine print — and be wary of people asking for upfront fees.
- Reporting Requirements – At the time of this publication, NIL GO and Deloitte support the reporting of deals valued at $600 or more. Expect this reporting process to become more standardized as NIL matures.

- Keep Compliance in Mind – Once your athlete is committed to a school, NIL activity must typically be reported to that school's compliance office.

3. Financial Literacy & Planning

Another important concept to understand is the difference between revenue sharing and third-party NIL money. Revenue sharing refers to income distributed by schools or conferences directly to athletes as part of a structured program, while third-party NIL money comes from businesses, brands, or individuals outside the school environment. Parents and athletes should know which type of NIL money is being discussed, as each has different compliance, tax, and reporting considerations.

NIL can be a powerful teacher of real-world money skills — but only if parents guide wisely:

- Track Income – Keep a record of every NIL payment. The IRS will expect taxes on this money.
- Budget Wisely – Teach your athlete to save, not just spend. Encourage them to set aside a portion for taxes, training, and future needs.
- Think Long-Term – Strongly consider working with a Certified Financial Planner (CFP) or licensed financial advisor. NIL earnings can be used to set up retirement or investment accounts early, establishing long-term financial health and teaching athletes the importance of responsible investing.

Families may also want to consider creating a business entity/structure. Simply put, setting up an entity (like an LLC or electing S-Corp status later) can offer some big advantages over taking income in your athlete's personal name. It offers liability protection, tax efficiency, professionalism, and long-term flexibility.

Action Steps for Parents Right Now

- Research your state's NIL rules for high school athletes
- Start a simple spreadsheet to track potential NIL deals
- Talk to your athlete about taxes and saving
- Help them define their personal brand — what do they want to stand for?
- Consider signing up for NIL Athlete Connect to be ready for legitimate opportunities as soon as they're available

Parent Tip: NIL isn't just about making money — it's about teaching your athlete to manage their reputation, negotiate, and think like an entrepreneur. With the right guidance, NIL can set them up for success far beyond their playing career.

Chapter 5
The Recruiting Process & Key Milestones

---·---

Nick Saban teaches that the path to success begins not with what you want to accomplish, but with how you plan to do it, one step at a time. The recruiting process is exciting — but it can feel like a marathon of decisions, deadlines, and travel. Breaking it down year by year helps parents and athletes know what to focus on at each stage.

1. Freshman Year (9th Grade): Foundation Building

- Focus on Academics – Every class counts toward NCAA eligibility. Start strong.
- Athletic Development – Build strength, speed, and positional skills.
- Film & Exposure – Begin collecting game film — even JV film matters.
- Camps – Attend developmental camps to improve skills, not to be "seen."

2. Sophomore Year (10th Grade): Early Awareness

- Grades & Testing – Stay on top of GPA. Consider taking the PSAT.

- Find out your school's early graduation requirements.
- Varsity Film – If on varsity, create first highlight reel.
- Communication – Your athlete can begin sending intro emails to coaches with GPA, measurables, and Hudl link.
- Camps – Selectively attend 2-3 local and/or regional camps or combines to get verified measurables. If appropriate attend a mega-camp as there will be many schools in attendance.
- Family Observation – Begin to watch how your athlete handles pressure, competition, and communication. Coaches notice these traits early.

3. Junior Year (11th Grade): Prime Recruiting Window

- Standardized Tests – Take SAT/ACT early to allow time for retakes.
- Film Updates – Share mid-season highlight reels with coaches.
- Attend Junior Day visits – these events give athletes and families a closer look at a program's culture, facilities, and coaching staff, and signal which recruits schools are most serious about.
- Camps & Showcases – If your athlete performs exceptionally well at a major showcase (Under Armour, Rivals, etc.), it can sometimes negate the need to attend multiple additional camps. Avoid overexposure — too many camps can lead to fatigue and risk of average performances, which may lower your ranking within your class or position. Choose your camp schedule wisely and strategically.
- Unofficial Visits – There is now no limit on the number of unofficial visits. Choose wisely — you are responsible for travel costs, so budget carefully and prioritize schools where there is real interest or a realistic fit. Consider only going to the schools that have your study major and offensive/defensive scheme that fit your athlete's particular skillset.

- In-Person Impressions – Visits allow programs to see how your athlete — and your family — carry themselves. Coaches watch how parents interact, how questions are asked, and how the family supports (or pressures) the athlete.
- See Operations Up Close – Visiting during spring practice or offseason workouts helps you evaluate team culture and coaching style beyond game-day hype.

4. Senior Year (12th Grade): Decision Time

- Film – Share early-season senior highlights promptly.
- Official Visits – Use these for top choices where there is real mutual interest.
- Cost Awareness – Official visits are covered by the school, but unofficial visits remain self-funded — plan accordingly.
- Family Representation – How your family shows up matters. Coaches want to see parents and guardians who will be partners, not problems.
- Decision & Signing Day – Communicate respectfully with all programs — even those you decline. Celebrate the milestone with humility and gratitude.

Key Takeaways

- You Don't Have to Do Everything – Performing well at a big camp can check the box — don't chase every event.
- Be Strategic About Exposure – Overexposure or mediocre performances can hurt rankings. Quality > quantity.
- In-Person Interaction is Crucial – Programs want to see your athlete live and observe your family dynamic.
- Your Family is Part of the Package – Coaches are evaluating the environment their recruit will come from. Show respect, professionalism, and partnership.

Chapter 6
Life After the Commitment

'Twas the night before Commitment Day, and I remembered a great suggestion shared by another parent during one of Riley's official visits. A mom told me how her son had called each coach who recruited him to thank them personally for their time, the offer, and their investment in his journey — but also to let them know he'd chosen a different program.

It sounded like such a respectful way to close the chapter — and in football, where the world is small and paths cross often, leaving bridges intact can matter down the road. So, I advised Riley to do the same.

He went upstairs and called the first coach.

That first call did not go well. In fact, it went terribly! The conversation ended with the program asking Riley not to announce his decision, requesting a Zoom call with all of us, and even prompting Riley to blurt out — prematurely — where he had chosen to commit. We decided not to call any other programs until after the commitment announcement was public.

Even so, I still believe this can be a meaningful way to close the process — as long as you prepare your athlete for the possibility of an emotional response and handle it with grace.

1. Early Graduation & Early Enrollment

One of the most significant decisions your family may face after committing is whether your athlete should graduate early from high school and enroll in college in January rather than the following summer.
Pros:

- Head Start on Development – Participate in spring football, learn the playbook, and get a jump on strength and conditioning.
- Academic Advantage – Adjust to college coursework before the season starts.
- Depth Chart Opportunity – Early enrollees are often more prepared by fall camp.

Cons:

- Rushed Senior Year – Your athlete may miss prom, spring sports, or other milestones.
- Emotional Readiness – Some athletes aren't ready to leave home early.
- Logistics – Not all high schools allow early graduation and credit requirements may require summer or online classes.

How Common:

Early graduation is common at Power 5 programs, where many signees are expected to be on campus in January. Smaller programs may not offer it.

2. Closing Out the Recruiting Process

- Communicating Decisions – Calling or texting coaches to thank them is professional and respectful — but timing matters. Consider waiting until after the public announcement to avoid misunderstandings.
- Leaving No Bridges Burned – Today's "No" could become tomorrow's transfer destination or graduate school program.

3. Academic Readiness

- Stay Focused Until Graduation – Offers can be rescinded if grades slip. Finish strong.
- College Preparation – Build consistent study habits now.
- Eligibility Center – Double-check that transcripts and NCAA paperwork are complete.

4. Physical Preparation

- Strength & Conditioning – Complete summer workout packets — incoming athletes are tested.
- Nutrition – Dial in fueling and hydration habits early.
- Injury Prevention – Resolve nagging injuries before reporting.

5. Mental & Emotional Preparation

- Role Adjustment – Your athlete may go from star player to a freshman fighting for reps.
- Support & Mental Health – Normalize conversations about homesickness and mental health.

6. Parent & Family Role

- Healthy Boundaries – Let your athlete advocate for themselves.
- Team Support – Show up positively on game day.
- Avoiding Overreach – Refrain from contacting coaches about playing time.

7. NIL & Financial Life

- Compliance – Report NIL deals through the school's process.
- Budgeting – Teach money management.

- Planning Ahead – Discuss savings and long-term goals.

8. Growth Beyond Football

- Career Development – Encourage internships and networking.
- Celebrate Milestones – Recognize first snaps and achievements.
- Perspective – Help your athlete focus on who they are becoming.

Key Takeaways

- Close with Class – End the recruiting journey respectfully.
- Prepare for Transition – Academic, physical, and emotional readiness are critical.
- Support Without Smothering – Parents transition from advocates to advisors.

Closing Note

While this playbook is designed to serve as a resource and guide, there is no guarantee that following these steps will result in an athletic scholarship, an offer to play at the next level, or an opportunity at your athlete's dream school. Every athlete's journey is unique, and outcomes will vary. At the end of the day, your athlete's talent, discipline, and passion for the game will be the major driving forces behind their success. Use this playbook and resources as tools to stay organized and informed, but never lose sight of the bigger picture! As we often remind our own son, Riley, who is now playing at The Ohio State University: keep the main thing the main thing.

The following resources are provided to help you and your athlete stay organized and confident through the process:

Football Program Comparison Worksheet

Print and use this worksheet to compare schools based on city/town, travel ease, academic support, coaches, strength program, position depth, plan for development, conference strength, NIL opportunities, and game-day atmosphere.

Unofficial Visit Questions

Comprehensive list of questions to ask during unofficial visits, focusing on academics, program culture, and player development.

Official Visit Preparation Checklist

Step-by-step checklist covering attire, logistics, mindset, and follow-up actions to get the most out of official visits.

Official Visit Question Guide

In-depth guide to questions about player development, scheme fit, coaching style, expectations, accountability, and NIL (if offered).

Unofficial Visit Question Guide

Unofficial visits are a valuable way to see a program up close and meet coaches and players. Since you cover your own costs, you'll want to budget accordingly and make each visit count. Below is a curated set of questions based on key areas to evaluate during your visit.

⚠ Important: Avoid asking NIL questions during unofficial visits if your athlete has not yet received an offer. Focus instead on academics, culture, development, and overall fit.

Recruiting

- How does the program/coach view and use the transfer portal, and how does that affect roster spots at my athlete's position?
- How many scholarship-athletes are typically offered in my athlete's position group each year?

Academic Support & Development

- What majors work best with the football schedule?
- What kind of academic support (tutors, study halls, advisors) is provided?
- How do you help athletes who struggle academically? How do you support athletes who wish to pursue more challenging areas of study,

such as STEM majors or double majors, while balancing athletic commitments?

- Are there specific GPA or credit hour requirements to stay eligible?

Football Culture & Coaching Philosophy

- How would you describe the culture of this program?
- What qualities do you value most in players — on and off the field?
- How do you approach player development (strength, skills, leadership)?
- What does a typical day look like during the season and offseason?
- How do you handle discipline or conflict within the team?

What are your personal and professional goals for the next 2–3 years, and how do you see those aligning with the direction of the program?

Strength, Conditioning & Health

- What does your strength program look like during offseason vs. in-season?
- What resources do you have for injury prevention and rehab?
- How do you individualize workouts for each position group?
- Is there a nutritionist or fueling station available to players?

Facilities & Resources

- Can we tour the training rooms, weight room, and academic facilities?
- What new upgrades or renovations are planned in the next few years?
- How accessible are athletic trainers, mental health resources, and medical staff?

Player Experience & Locker Room Culture

- Can we meet current players or have a candid conversation with them?
- How do players describe life in this program — on and off the field?
- How does the team handle redshirting, position changes, or transfers?
- What support exists for freshmen during the transition to college?

Game Day & Community Atmosphere

- What is the game day atmosphere like here?
- How involved is the local community with the program?
- Are there traditions that make this program special?

Family & Communication

- How do coaches prefer to communicate with parents?
- Are parents welcome to attend certain practices, meetings, or events?
- What role do you expect families to play in supporting their athletes?

Preparing for Official Visits Parent & Athlete Checklist

---•---

Official visits are part interview, part audition, and part celebration. Your family is representing your athlete — and your athlete is representing themselves. Here's how to make sure you're ready!

1. Wardrobe & Appearance

- Athlete Attire – Comfortable but presentable for campus tours (athletic wear, not pajamas). Bring good walking shoes — slides may be fine for travel, but sneakers are best in case a coach asks you to participate or demo.
- Evening Casual Outfit – Nice jeans, polo/shirt, or casual dress for dinners.
- Parent Attire – Casual or Athleisure for meetings and meals. Comfortable shoes for walking but avoid overly casual looks. Keep it classy!

2. Pre-Visit Preparation

- Review athlete's Hudl/film to be ready if asked to discuss strengths and goals.
- Research the program's record, roster, and depth chart.

- Prioritize questions from your Official Visit Question Guide.
- Prepare respectful, professional social media posts.

3. Travel & Logistics

- Double-check flights, hotel details, and transportation.
- Bring ID, required paperwork, and any forms provided by the program.
- Pack toiletries, medications, and weather-appropriate clothes.
- Confirm who is invited (parents, guardians, siblings).

4. Mindset & Etiquette

- Be engaged — phones away during coach meetings, meals, and presentations.
- Be polite and approachable with staff, players, and other recruits.
- Encourage your athlete to speak for themselves (shake hands, make eye contact).
- Parents — ask questions, but avoid dominating conversations.

5. After the Visit

- Debrief as a family right after: what felt right, any red flags?
- Fill out your Program Comparison Worksheet while impressions are fresh.
- Send a thank-you message (athlete first, parents optional) within 24–48 hours.

Official Visit Question Guide

Official visits are your opportunity to go deeper — to get clear on how your athlete will fit into a program, both on and off the field. These questions help you understand development plans, scheme fit, expectations, and the coaching philosophy of the staff.

Athletic & Player Development

- Where do you see my athlete fitting in your depth chart in Year 1 and beyond?
- Do you project my athlete as a starter, rotational player, or developmental prospect?
- What is your track record for developing players at this position for the next level?
- Can you share examples of past players who had a similar build/skillset and how they were used?
- How often do you evaluate and adjust training plans for individual needs?

Scheme & Role Fit

- What base offense/defense do you run, and how do you see my athlete fitting within that scheme?

- How much flexibility do players have to cross-train or move between positions?

- Are there opportunities for early playing time, or will my athlete likely redshirt?

- What does your ideal player at this position look like physically and mentally?

Coaching & Teaching Style

- How do you teach and install the playbook — classroom, video sessions, walk-throughs?

- How do you handle mistakes on the field or in practice?

- What kind of feedback style should my athlete expect — direct, detailed, tough love, encouraging?

- What are your professional or career goals over the next 2–3 years, and how do they align with the program's vision and stability?

- What is your approach to leadership development (captains, mentoring younger players)?

Expectations & Accountability

- What does the offseason schedule look like (workouts, meetings, film study)?

- What are expectations for weight training, nutrition, and study hall participation?

- How do you track player progress — physically, mentally, and academically?

- What support do you provide for time management and balancing academics with athletics?

Team Culture & Locker Room

- How do you maintain a strong culture year after year?

- What qualities do your current leaders possess that you'd like my athlete to develop?
- How do you support freshmen and transfers through the transition?

Family & Communication

- How do you communicate with parents during the season (injuries, depth chart updates, etc.)?
- What do you expect from families in terms of involvement and game-day support?

NIL (If Offered)

- Does the school provide education or compliance support for NIL deals?
- Are there collectives or resources available to help athletes find opportunities?
- How do you ensure NIL opportunities do not interfere with academics or team obligations?

Football Program Comparison Worksheet

*Rate each category for each school on a scale of 1-3: 1 (Could Be Better), 2 (Solid), 3 (Excellent).

Category	School 1	School 2	School 3	School 4	School 5	School 6	School 7	School 8	School 9	School 10
City/Town/Campus Likability										
Travel Ease										
Field of Study/Academic Support										
Head Coach										
Coordinator										
Position Coach										
Strength & Nutrition Program										
Depth of Position Room										
Plan for Development/Use										
Strength of Conference/Schedule										
NIL Opportunities										
Gameday Atmosphere										

TOTAL SCORE: _______________________

AVERAGE (1-3): _______________________

Visit Notes

About the Authors

Duke Pettijohn is a former standout defensive end at Syracuse University and a veteran of the NFL & AFL. His passion for football has always gone beyond playing — it's a true love for the game itself. After his professional career, Duke has continued devoting himself to coaching and mentoring young athletes of all ages, pouring that same passion into helping them sharpen their skills, grow as teammates, and develop the character they need to succeed both on and off the field.

Juliet Jones Pettijohn is a former biopharma executive turned entrepreneur and founder of **NIL Athlete Connect**, a platform designed to help families navigate the evolving NIL space responsibly. She deeply enjoyed walking alongside her son Riley through the recruiting process, learning valuable lessons from coaches, general managers, and fellow parents. That journey not only expanded her knowledge of the game but also inspired her to create resources that empower other families to approach recruiting with confidence.

Together, Duke and Juliet are the proud parents of three children – Duke, Riley, and Sloane. Their personal journey as football parents, combined with their professional experiences, inspired them to create this resource. Fourth and

Goal: A Recruiting Playbook for Football Parents reflects their commitment to equipping families with the tools, questions, and perspective needed to support their student-athletes' success — both on and off the field.

To learn more about NIL Athlete Connect, visit www.nilathleteconnect.com:

- **Education & Guidance** – Helping athletes and families understand NIL opportunities and responsibilities.
- **Brand Connections** – Linking athletes with authentic partnerships that align with their values.
- **Earnings Support** – Tools to explore potential compensation while encouraging responsible participation.
- **Insights & Tracking** – Clear analytics to monitor engagement, growth, and campaign performance.
- **Family Resources** – Practical strategies for communication, financial literacy, and long-term planning.